I0810806

IN FOCUS: NATIVE AMERICANS

APACHE

HISTORY AND CULTURE

MARK STEWART

Cavendish Square

Published in 2026 by Cavendish Square Publishing, LLC
2544 Clinton Street, Buffalo, NY 14224

Website: cavendishsq.com

Portions of this work were originally authored by Wren Richmond and published as *Apache* (Spotlight on Native Americans). All new material this edition authored by Mark Stewart.

Publisher: Katie Kawa
Book Design: Lisa Miley

Portions of this work were reviewed by: Robert J. Conley, Former Sequoyah Distinguished Professor at Western Carolina University and Director of Native American Studies at Morningside College and Montana State University.

Photo Credits: Carol Highsmith/Library of Congress (4*, 18*); John F. Huckel/Cornell University Library (5*); K.T. Dodge/Library of Congress (6*); C.S. Fly (7*); Peter Newark's American Pictures (8); Frederic Remington (9*, 15*); Detroit Photographic Co. (11*); Edward Curtis/Library of Congress (12*, 16*); Apache Tribe/San Carlos, Arizona (13 top*); National Park Service (13 bottom*, 24, 29); C.C. Pierce/ Doheny Memorial Library (14*);National Archives (17*); Carlisle Indian School Digital Resource Center (19); Native Stock (20, 21, 29); Becka M. Photography (22); Apache Tribe of Oklahoma (23); Anders Ryman/Native Stock (26); Moz Designs (27); Peter Turnley/Corbis/VCG via Getty Images (28).

Cover images (clockwise from top): Frederic Remington*; Peter Turnley/Corbis/VCG via Getty Images; C.S. Fly*; Edward Curtis/Library of Congress*; Native Stock; Author's Collection.

*These images are in the public domain

Cataloging-in-Publication Data
Names: Stewart, Mark, 1960 July 7-.
Title: Apache history and culture / Mark Stewart.
Description: Buffalo, NY : Cavendish Square Publishing, 2026. | Series: In focus: Native Americans| Includes glossary and index.
Identifiers: ISBN 9781502674913 (pbk.) | ISBN 9781502674920 (library bound) | ISBN 9781502674937 (ebook)
Subjects: LCSH: Apache Indians--Juvenile literature. | Indians of North America--Juvenile literature. | Indigenous peoples--Social life and customs--Juvenile literature.
Classification: LCC E99.A6 S94 2026 | DDC 979.0049725--dc23

CPSIA compliance information: Batch #CS26CSQ: For further information contact Cavendish Square Publishing LLC at 1-877-980-4450.
Printed in the United States of America

CONTENTS

ABOUT OUR GLOSSARY

In this book, there may be several words or terms you are reading for the first time, or words that are familiar but used in an unusual way. All of these words appear in **bold type** throughout the book and are defined on page 30.

I AM THE LAND

The American Southwest is the hottest, driest region of the United States. Although it includes many different **ecosystems**, all feature high temperatures and low rainfall. Despite the challenges of climate, humans have lived in the deserts, **plateaus**, and mountains of the Southwest for more than 10,000 years. The Apache people were not the first to build a life in this part of the world, but they were among the most successful. Their territory included parts of Arizona, Colorado, New Mexico, Oklahoma, Texas, and northern Mexico. For many years, this was known as Apacheria.

The Apaches have occupied this land for at least 700 years. In the 1300s, a decades-long drought forced

This painting shows an Apache war party on the move.

agricultural societies to abandon their towns and villages. The Apaches were one of the tribes that filled this **void**. Some scholars believe they arrived 500 years earlier. They took what their harsh environment offered and built a culture that enabled them to survive and thrive.

For hundreds of years, a large part of Apache territory included the southern part of the Great Plains. This area was home to millions of bison and was fertile enough to do limited farming. During the 1700s, the Apaches fought and lost a war with the Comanches for

◀ The challenges of the hot, dry Southwest environment have shaped Apache history and culture for centuries.

control over the southern Great Plains. Most were forced to move further south and west into the drier mountains and deserts. These groups are known collectively as the Western Apaches. One band joined the Kiowa tribe, while another moved south to Texas. These groups are known collectively as the Eastern Apaches.

Even so, the Apache tribe adapted extremely well to the various features of their territory. Because resources were often limited, it did not make sense to construct large, permanent villages. They tended to live in small settlements with only a handful of related families. Over time, individual bands developed—some in the mountains, some in the open desert, others in

valleys and canyons—with slight differences in customs and language.

All hunted wild game and collected wild plants for food and medicine. Some engaged in limited farming. They were a mobile people who followed the migratory path of animals and moved with the changing seasons. They were careful not to take all the food in one area for fear that it might not recover in time for their return. One of the Apaches' greatest skills was knowing when and where they could access water. They depended on hidden springs and knew the locations of the **dry washes** where water accumulated after it rained.

◀ Ceremonial dances have been a key part of Apache culture for centuries. This photo shows tribe members performing the Devil Dance.

The tribe's name—"Apache"—came from the Zuni word *apachu*, which means "enemy." Spanish settlers heard this word and it went into common use. The Apaches call themselves *Indé* (or *Nde*), which means "the people." The Apachean language is a branch of the Southern **Athabaskan** family, which developed in the northwestern region of the continent. There are five main **dialects** of Apache.

FIRST CONTACT

When European explorers first arrived in the Southwest in 1540, the Apaches were still lords of the southern Great Plains. They hunted bison and held annual trade fairs with the Pueblo people to the south, where they exchanged meat and hides for corn, tools, pottery, and other necessities. When the Spanish imposed taxes on the Pueblos, it left them with little to trade. This was

This painting shows the arrival of Spanish soldiers in the 1540s. More than 300 years of conflict followed.

a major blow to the Apache economy.

As more and more Spanish settlements were built, the Apaches targeted them for raids. The horses acquired in these raids increased the mobility of the Apaches. For more than two centuries, they were a thorn in the side of the Spanish government—so much so that other tribes were sometimes paid to fight against them.

After having been driven off their most prized land by the Comanches, the Apaches held on to what remained with incredible **tenacity**. After gaining independence from Spain in 1821, Mexico moved against the Apaches. In 1835, the Mexican government placed a **bounty** on Apache scalps to encourage people to kill them. During the 1800s, the Apaches opposed settlers from Mexico, the **Republic of Texas**, and the United States, becoming one of the most feared and respected tribes in the Southwest.

Apache raids on Spanish settlements often focused on obtaining horses.

I AM A WARRIOR

The Apache warrior was a master of **stealth**. From an early age, boys learned how to conceal themselves and disappear into their surrounding environment. This was not only important in battle, but in hunting, as well. Apaches were especially good at setting up ambushes and launching surprise attacks, seemingly appearing out of nowhere. A small group of warriors, concealed in a rocky pass, could hold off ten times their number.

Training for a young Apache warrior also included building up speed and **endurance**. They were able to move rapidly over long distances with little water. In battle, their quickness and agility enabled them to outrun horses in thick vegetation. In close combat, their strength and endurance was almost always superior to that of their enemies—especially European soldiers, who were more dependent on horses and firearms to gain an advantage. Once the Apaches acquired these, their hit-and-run **guerilla warfare** tactics became almost unstoppable.

Three Apache warriors are shown with their weapons.

Weapons for fighting and hunting included the bow and arrow, spears, **lances**, and tomahawks, as well as shields for protection. Apache warriors were especially good when it came to fighting with knives. They practiced this skill from an early age, perfecting fast, precise movements that made them quiet and effective killers. A major prize in Apache raids was the hunting rifle. Whether firing at game or at their enemies, warriors were excellent shots. They controlled their horses with their leg and body movements, freeing up both hands to use their weapons.

During the 1800s, several Apache battle leaders gained fame throughout the nation for their skill and daring. Mangas Coloradas, a Central Apache tribal chief, defeated soldiers from Mexico time and again. In 1846, he supported the United States in its war with Mexico—but later fought against American forces. His son-in-law, Cochise, a Chiricahua Apache, stood at least six feet tall and fought soldiers on both sides of the U.S.-Mexico border.

▲ An Apache warrior draws his bow.

Geronimo, a Ndendahe Apache, organized raids with other Apache bands against U.S. and Mexican settlements starting as a young man in the 1850s. Geronimo had great hatred for all Mexicans, whose soldiers massacred his family. He and his warriors rarely left a Mexican alive after a raid.

Although Apache culture had strict gender roles, not all of their leaders were men. Lozen, a warrior, medicine woman, and prophet, was **revered** for her courage and cunning. It was said that she possessed supernatural powers that enabled her to predict the movements of Apache enemies. The second person on the right in the back row is the only known photo of Lozen.

◀ This photo shows the famous warrior Geronimo in 1905, when he was more than 75 years old.

A NEW REALITY

At the start of America's war with Mexico in 1846, Mangas Coloradas granted the U.S. Army safe passage through Apache territory and later signed a peace treaty. That peace lasted until miners, ranchers, and farmers began flooding into Apache lands during the 1850s. When violence erupted, the government decided that the Apache threat had to be eliminated.

The United States built forts to fight the Apache and sent thousands of soldiers to enforce the tribe's relocation to reservations—including some that were not even on traditional Apache territory. A series of major conflicts cost countless lives on both sides and saw some of the most brutal fighting in American history. These became known as the Apache Wars.

Apaches began to accept reservation life in the early 1870s. After

Reservation life was hard on the Apache people. It disrupted their traditional ways.

This painting shows American soldiers fleeing from an Apache war party.

thriving for centuries as a nomadic people, the Apaches found the reservation system to be disruptive to their culture and traditions. The food and supplies promised by the U.S. government did not always materialize, leading to hunger and sickness, which undercut the **prestige** and authority of tribal leaders.

At various times during the 1870s and 1880s, Apache bands broke out and staged raids in U.S. and Mexican territories, knowing that each nation's pursuit had to stop at the border between the two countries. Their aim was to return their people to a traditional lifestyle. The last holdout was Geronimo, whose legendary resistance made him an international celebrity.

BEING APACHE

For hundreds of years, the Apache people were spread over a huge **swath** of the Southwest. Over time and distance, more than a dozen different groups developed. While each had different customs and spoke different dialects of the Athabaskan language, they shared much in common. For example, an Apache encampment would likely be made up of extended family members—and be one of many in a particular area, all bound by family ties and guided by a chief who was selected for his leadership qualities.

After marriage, a young man would go to live with his wife's mother's family and become a member of her **clan**. This type of structure is known as matrilineal. Interestingly, an Apache mother was discouraged from communicating directly with her son-in-law in the spirit of avoiding conflict.

Apache mothers kept their infants safe on cradleboards while doing their work.

A group of Apaches pose in front of structures called wickiups, which provided shelter and blended in with the landscape.

The division of labor in Apache society was typical of many Native American tribes. Men hunted, raided, and fought their enemies, while women gathered local plants, prepared food, reared children, and made baskets and other household items. Where farming was possible, everyone pitched in. Although women did not hold the position of chief, they played an important leadership role and also acted as **shamans**.

Apache children were thrown into survival training shortly after they were old enough to walk. Each morning at sunrise, boys and girls were sent running to the top

of a hill and back. As they grew older, they were required to carry a mouthful of water the whole way without losing any. On winter mornings, they would be made to roll naked in the snow. By the time they were teenagers, they had learned to withstand cold, heat, hunger, and thirst that few other humans could endure. They developed speed and **stamina**

An Apache mother and daughter pose for the camera. Young boys and girls underwent similar survival training.

through footraces. These races are still an important part of annual Apache gatherings, most notably among the Jicarilla Apaches and Mescalero Apaches in New Mexico.

Eastern Apaches lived in tipis (tepees) made of bison hides. After losing their hunting grounds to the Comanches, they simply traded for the hides they needed. Western Apaches lived in wickiups, which were made by creating a round frame with branches and then covered with desert bushes and leaves. Wickiups provided much-needed shade in the desert heat and had the added advantage of blending into the landscape. This made Apache encampments difficult to find.

One of the most heartbreaking aspects of Apache reservation life was the break-up of families through government boarding schools, such as the Carlisle Indian School in Pennsylvania. Students were stripped of their culture and prohibited from speaking their Native language.

SOMETHING SACRED

Like many Native American cultures, the Apaches believe in a supreme being, who created the world and the first humans. A female **deity**, Changing Woman, plays a key role in their origin stories. As her name implies, she possesses the power to change her appearance, growing old in the winter and young in the spring. She symbolizes the cycles of nature and **fertility**, and is honored in ceremonies celebrating childbirth, marriage, and young women's coming of age. Changing Woman gave birth to two

The Mountain Spirit Dance is performed to protect the Apache people from disease and enemies. Ceremonies like this are an important part of spiritual life.

Painted hides, like this one by Joseph Skywolf, are sometimes used to record legends and stories. This is one way that art and tradition are linked in Apache culture.

sons, Monster Slayer and Child of Water, who made the world safe for people.

The concept of death in Apache culture was complex. The deceased were buried with their possessions and then moved on to the "Land of Endless Summer." However, grieving rituals could last many months. It was not unusual for a family to move after the death of a loved one in order to avoid that person's ghost and they tried not to mention his or her name. Following the death of a parent, children might change their name to avoid the sadness of remembering how their parents used it.

Apaches even avoided *talking* about death. If the topic came up during planning for a raid or war party, it was likely to be cancelled. And although Apache storytelling featured many different animals, it did not include owls, because it was believed that the birds were the ghosts of the departed. The hooting of an owl within earshot of an Apache camp could cause great concern.

Apache cultural and spiritual traditions have inspired many creative works over the past century. The poetry of Roman C. Adrian, a White Mountain Apache, has appeared in many publications, including *The Remembered Earth*, the first major collection of Native American literature, published in 1979. More recently, Darcie Little Badger, a Lipan Apache,

Darcie Little Badger draws on her Apache heritage to create fantasy and science fiction known as Indigenous Futurism.

had written fantasy and science fiction stories that feature characters drawn from Apache and other Native American cultures. She is one of the leading authors in an exciting **literary genre** called Indigenous Futurism.

Another inventive writer is Julian Talamantez Broslaski, whose family includes members of the Lipan and Mescalero tribes. He released his third critically acclaimed book of poetry in 2023 and is also a talented musical performer who sets his unique lyrics to classic melodies inspired by country and western songs.

Apache tribes and reservations are now scattered across Arizona, New Mexico, Oklahoma, and Texas, as well as four states in northern Mexico. In the United States, there are 13 Apache tribes: Chiricahua, Cibecue, Jicarilla, Kiowa, Lipan, Mescalero, Northern Tonto, Southern Tonto, San Carlos, White Mountain, and Yavani.

PAST, PRESENT, FUTURE

According to a survey completed in 2022, more than 70,000 people are part of the different Apache nations. The two largest tribes are the San Carlos Apaches and White Mountain Apaches, with a total population of more than 30,000. Both reservations are located in New Mexico and they are considered part of the Western Apaches.

The San Carlos Apache Reservation spans 1.8 million acres (728,434 h) in southwest Arizona. The tribe—whose territory once touched parts of California and Texas—operates a number of businesses related to tourism,

This bust of the famed Chiricahua leader Cochise greets visitors at a national park in Arizona. It celebrates the history and heritage of the Apache people.

An Eastern Apache drummer keeps time during a ceremonial dance.

including two casinos. One of its holiest sites, Chi'chil Bildagoteel (also known as Oak Flat), sits atop one of North America's largest copper deposits. In 2014, Congress approved a bill transferring this land to two international mining companies. Apache groups opposed the deal in court and brought their fight to the United Nations in 2023.

The White Mountain Apache Reservation covers 1.67 million acres (675,825 h) in east-central Arizona. It is a popular hunting, fishing, and camping destination, with

400 miles (644 km) of streams and an incredible diversity of wildlife. The tribe manages these recreational lands, which are an important part of its economy. Among its success stories is the return of the Apache trout, which was once on the brink of extinction. The White Mountain Apaches also operate a casino and ski resort. Its reservation includes

The casino in Lawton, Oklahoma, is one of several businesses operated by the Apache people.

Mount Baldy, which is Arizona's second-highest peak at 11,421 feet (3,481 m)—and also a sacred site for the tribe.

The Eastern Apache groups include the Mescalero, Jicarilla, Chiricahua, Lipan, and Kiowa-Apaches. Their economies include ranching, farming, lumber, mining, and tourism. Casinos operated by the Jicarilla and Mescalero Nations are important sources of income and employment for tribal members. The Fort Sill Apache Tribe—which is made up of four different bands of

◀ A statue of an Apache warrior overlooks a golf course on the San Carlos Reservation. Recreational visitors make up an important part of tourism.

Chirachua Apaches—operates a casino in Lawton, Oklahoma.

Apache governments provide their people with a range of basic services, from law enforcement to education to healthcare. Each faces the challenge of creating economic opportunities for its people, as well as preserving its language, heritage, and culture.

Throughout history, the Apache tribe was made up of different people living in different places, but with many common cultural and spiritual beliefs. Today, the distinct Apache groups in the United States and Mexico still share important traditions.

◀ A Mescalero Apache man competes in the annual Fashion and Designer Challenge held in Santa Fe, New Mexico. Attending Native American festivals is one of the many ways the Apache people share their culture and traditions.

GLOSSARY AND FURTHER READING

GLOSSARY

Athabaskan—A family of Indigenous languages originating in the western part of North America.

Bounty—A sum paid for the capture or killing of another person.

Clan—A close-knit extended family related by kinship or common ancestors.

Deity—A god or supernatural being that is worshiped by people.

Dialects—Slightly different forms of the same language.

Dry Washes—Narrow stream beds that only flow during periods of rain. Sometimes these are called arroyos.

Ecosystems—Groups of living and non-living things that create nutrients and energy within different areas.

Endurance—The ability to do something difficult for a long time.

Fertility—The natural ability for people, plants, and animals to reproduce.

Guerilla Warfare—A type of combat using small groups of fighters. Guerilla is Spanish for "little war."

Lances—Spear-like weapons used by mounted warriors.

Literary Genre—A category of writing that shares specific characteristics, such as science fiction or romance.

Plateaus—Large areas of level high ground.

Prestige—Widespread admiration.

Republic of Texas—An independent nation that existed in current-day Texas between 1836 and 1846.

Revered—Deeply respected and admired.

Shamans—Tribe members with access to the spirit world.

Stamina—The ability to keep from tiring.

Stealth—Being quiet, cautious, and sneaky.

Swath—A long, wide strip of territory.

Tenacity—Great determination.

Void—An empty space.

BOOKS

Krupat, Arnold. *Boarding School Voices: Carlisle Indian School Students Speak*. Lincoln, NE: University of Nebraska Press, 2021.

Rossiter, Brienna. *The Trail of Tears.* Mendota Heights, MN: North Star Editions, 2025.

Tyler, Ron. *Native Americans: The Complete Plates of McKenney, Catlin, and Bodmer.* Cologne, Germany: Taschen America, 2024.

Various Authors. *My Life: Growing Up Native in America.* New York, NY: MTV Books/Simon & Schuster Children's Publishing, 2024.

ABOUT THE AUTHOR

MARK STEWART has written more than 150 non-fiction books for educational publishers, covering history, sports, and popular culture. His family tree tells a complex story common to many Americans. Mark's ancestors include some of the first European colonists, as well as the Indigenous people with whom early settlers interacted. Some faced off on the field of battle while others fought side-by-side. His 10th great-grandfather was **Myles Standish**, an officer on the ***Mayflower***, while his ninth great-grandmother was **Singing Bird Corbison**, who was described as a "Shawnee woman" but who was probably from the **Wampanoag** tribe. The Wampanoag people saved Standish and his fellow **Pilgrims** from starvation during the winter of 1620–21, forming the basis for the story of Thanksgiving. The descendants of Corbison and Standish blended into a single family in 1789, and then headed west in search of opportunity. This brought Mark's ancestors into direct conflict with Native people along the frontier in the 1700s and 1800s. Mark's sixth great-grandmother recalled frantically casting bullets for her husband as they defended their small Kentucky fort from an attack. Another served under 23-year-old **Abraham Lincoln** in the Illinois Militia during the Black Hawk War of 1832. Mark's more recent ancestors chose to fight their battles with words—as writers and editors of books, newspapers, and magazines. In 2007, he authored a history of the **Indian Removal Act of 1830** and the infamous **Trail of Tears**.

INDEX